THE PERFECT ORCHESTRA

THE PERFECT ORCHESTRA

POEMS

MARCH 30 – JULY 25, 1988

DANIEL ABDAL-HAYY MOORE

The Ecstatic Exchange

2009

Philadelphia

The Perfect Orchestra
Copyright © 2009 Daniel Abdal-Hayy Moore
All rights reserved.
Printed in the United States of America

For quotes any longer than those for critical articles and reviews,
contact:
The Ecstatic Exchange,
6470 Morris Park Road, Philadelphia, PA 19151-2403
email: abdalhayy@danielmoorepoetry.com

First Edition
ISBN: 978-0-578-02569-8 (paper)
Published by *The Ecstatic Exchange*,
6470 Morris Park Road, Philadelphia, PA 19151-2403

Also available from The Ecstatic Exchange:
Knocking from Inside, poems by Tiel Aisha Ansari

An earlier version of the poem *The Quest for Beauty* was originally
published in 1994 by Zilzal Press as a separate chapbook
illustrated by Sarah Steele.

Cover collage by the author
Back cover photograph by Peter Sanders

بسم الله الرحمن الرحيم

DEDICATION

To
Gene Gonder
first teacher and musical genius,
to Zen saint, Shunryu Suzuki,
to Shaykh ibn al-Habib
(and the continuation of the Habibiyya),
Shaykh Bawa Muhaiyuddeen,
all living and dead shuyukh of instruction and ma'arifa,
and to
Baji Tayyaba Khanum
of the unsounded depths

❖

The earth is not bereft
of Light

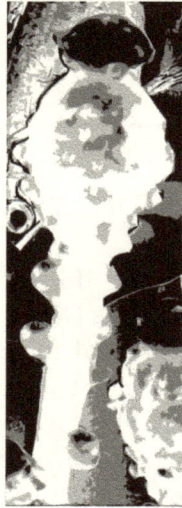

CONTENTS

PART 1
Author's Introduction   8
I Can Only Wait So Long   15
Bird Song   18
No Fixed Abode   21
Companion Moth   23
Glass Trumpet   24
We Can't Stop Singing   34
There's a Sunset Out There   36
Single Bird   39
If I Were to go to an Island   42
The Last Day   45

PART 2
Glinting Tip of Bird-Beak   61
The Natural Shape of Man   65
The Perfect Orchestra   69
The Initial Creational Gesture   80
Sitting As We Are   87
The Book is Everywhere   90
The Quest for Beauty   104
There's Something So Touching   121
I Had a Brief Intimation Tonight   124
Summer Night   127
The Darkness is a Tent of Mercy   146
Through the Latticework   150
Silence   152
After Reading This Last Poem   161

AUTHOR'S INTRODUCTION

I'm not sure why anyone would want to undergo spiritual training, the rigors and difficulties of a path of spiritual discipline, except to reach a state of enlightenment. And I'm not sure that the state of enlightenment would be one of grim survival, or a harsh stoicism after all the exhausting rigors, but rather a joyful and constant perception of the simultaneous multifariousness of all things and the single Divine core around which we all endlessly circulate. I'm not sure the so-called "death of the self" before our actual deaths would be like taking the wind out of our sails once and for all, or the fun out of our life because of fun's inherent evil, or the very existence of our identities somehow vampirised out of our ego beings, but rather a kind of percolatingly ecstatic and infinite vastness to all our actions and thoughts because our basest natures have been quieted, allowing original radiance to shine through. Because, in my life sitting with Zen Master Shunryu Suzuki for a couple of years, and then becoming a Muslim and lifelong adherent to a Sufi Tariqat beginning with Shaykh Muhammad ibn al Habib of Fez (may Allah be pleased with him), the point, through all the travails and historical shifts of the presentation of Islam since 1970 when I first embraced it, the point is not anything less than enlightenment, say what you will, the direct apprehension of the Divine Essence, the presence of eyewitnessing and the realization that "created beings are meanings projected in images," as the song of Shaykh ibn al-Habib so beautifully puts it.

Is this simply romantic, and is the peaceful joy we note in the faces and beings of the sainted ones real, and available to all of us, or only to the highly chosen and long-suffering (from the harshness of their discipline) few? God placed us on this earth, as we say, to worship Him, and some say that a symbiosis exists in which God created man *in order* to worship Him, and needs *us* to do so "in order to be known," as the Prophet Muhammad (peace be upon him) said of God in a famous Hadith Qudsi. But why did He create us unfinished, tempted, tempest-tossed from one thing to another, one moment sinning, the next moment repenting, as we swirl from relationships and successes and failures in this life? Are we all the prophet and Old Testament Job, diminished to sit among shards, diseased, bereft, patiently waiting for reprieve?

And finally what does the world of enlightenment look like? Is it then a blank screen entirely, one thing only and that one thing otherwordly? (Sensei Suzuki once sat with me in front of a giant blank screen that was hanging down in the auditorium of the first Zendo in San Francisco, and said that the mind was like that screen, and everything, all thoughts and desires, passed from one side to the other of it, and vanished away.) And if the goal of the Path is Allah, what does arrival (in this world, to say nothing of the next) look like?

The Perfect Orchestra, then, is the music that accompanies our journey, the very life of our life, breath of our breath and heartbeat of our heartbeat, this creation into which we've landed, willy-nilly, by the destiny of our births, high or low, pedigree or mutt, in joy or misery. It may be the "music of the spheres," or the very symphony around us and inside us simultaneously every moment, including the music in our dreams, the orchestra of God's compassionate Mercy every living moment of our lives, often muffled by the world around us, and needing our effort to listen intently to hear, though it be always with us and even audible to us, unheard.

This is it. That, as the Sufis and Zen Buddhists say and agree on, all knowledge is within us, and we need only to be re-enlightened to our original natures. The Voice of God and the voice within us, the voice of our mothers' tenderness and the loud rasp of tragedy that may befall us. Waterfalls and lightbulbs, doorknobs and avalanches, rivers and new shoes on hardwood. The fanfare of our births and the dirges of our deaths, and the raucous New Orleans Jazz band of our lives in-between.

And sensitivity to this orchestra? Is that a part of the Path to God? Are our senses heightened by their purification, so that we see and hear the vastness behind the details and then the sweetest and most perfect minutia of the total panorama? And is it more than a cliché to say that "everything is perfect as it is?" Isn't it? Are we being swindled? Are we simply ignorant, or so stuffed up with ourselves and our central importance to the drama of our lives that we cannot appreciate the perfection that is? Do we have to knock over the precious Ming vase of this life and break it into a thousand fragments and try to piece it back together to then see God's perfection everywhere?

The Perfect Orchestra of the Real. This world's natural light is supernatural light, and even when shining on the discordant, radiates calm, back to the central chord, the tonally harmonic resolution that laps throughout the universe as well as through us, end to end, and back again.

March 20, 2009

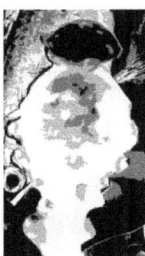

To the sane man the world is a musical instrument.
— Thoreau Journal (June 22, 1851)

PART 1

I CAN ONLY WAIT SO LONG

I can only wait so long
for the next song to come –

the house fills with smoke,
the hill the house sits on rises up on a

platter being carried by worms
into the presence of the King.

Out of the air, out of its
secret ovens, out of the

night with its
public noises, out of

earshot of cries and
shouts over the

stone bridge that crosses
Death River, howling like a

drunk banshee who's lost its
pack *(the moon looks*

good enough to
eat), out of the

rapid passing of things like targets at a
Penny Arcade but my

bee-bee gun's empty,
out of impatience to open lips wider than

the mouth of the Nile hidden in
secrecy, but whose watery speech is

obvious to Delta farmers whose
exotic crops thrive,

out of a bodily need to let inspiration originate from
various crannies of my body, from

leg-bones, ache in right shoulder, between
my legs where my

left heel is tucked, from the
high electric

sound in my
ears,

eye-dullness,
heartbeat gone too

long unheard, whose
record each new

poem is, like letting
sluice water out to

run down a

mountainside in

Peru to the patchwork of
parched fields below, using

Inca aqueducts the
moderns forgot while

starving,

out of a real hunger but with no real
giant's fist having come down on top of my head

as it so often does, with an
opening line or two, or a

title for a sequence, or a
vague but rhythmic

message forming like the
first curly head of a

newborn baby from the
mother's equally

curly-haired
opening into this world

emerging moist and almost with wings,

a song to sing!

3/30

BIRD SONG

I envy Olivier Messiaen
    stalking early mornings in the
      fields of France, in a
magazine article I saw
    years ago, with a

notebook, notating

      bird song!

He is said to be able to orchestrate birdcalls
just by hearing them, write those
    trills and
      watery runs with

tiny black dots on lines a musician back in a
musty room might play on his clarinet!

Notes, out of
    tree-wilderness, out of
      bird language, one to
          another for
      whatever reason, bodily
companionship, territorial
    rights, mating calls, thrills of
      pleasure in the plumage, beak

gabble, sunlight
    delirium, a bird's sense of

entertainment, some
    floating on updrafts,

whatever reasons God gives them for responding the
way God's made them
    respond over a

silken wheat field at
    first slants of
        dawn, gold

light along
dew blankets,

the world waking
  up, birds
 registering the
        waking,

Messiaen with his
stubby pencil attached like a

seismograph to the knowledge of his
    ear making

dots with or without little
black flags attached someone

back in a room can play on his
clarinet, or a

whole

orchestra, celestas, flutes, hitting those

high note-clusters, enraptured –

    for no reason!

                                      3/30

NO FIXED ABODE

With no fixed abode the thing floats in a
      blue frame, the alive
    presence that presents a
        face to us,
and we also, like sliding into a
      slide projector in which
 bright light is beamed
    through us from
    behind onto a
       blank screen, we also of

no fixed abode, but a series of
    moving still images en-
      livened by
Light,

and the plum hanging down over our
fence from the
plum tree, and it's this

delicate vibration in everything whose magnetic
    webs go always
      back to the
Source, and whose magnetic
fingertips, although at the uttermost extension, are
      actually from
first Source as well, of

no fixed abode, as if

striding into forms and
out again, cocked

hat, such a

hummingbird flutter of
        wings like
spirals out from the central
        body, not like
flapping, not like smooth
        usual flight,

this intangible thing we perceive by our acts of
        perception, glass held in the
            air, liquid
                held in the
                glass, light

held in the
liquid

shining
out!

                                            3/31

COMPANION MOTH

Companion moth on the
    wall by my pillow
late at
    night, facing the
lamp, with a
    small shadow your exact shape
tapered, cast behind.

When I turn to look again

you're gone.

4/4

GLASS TRUMPET

1

I want to blow high notes on a glass trumpet
that shows real things inside it, scenes of
objects and vistas all surrounded by very
matter-of-fact nimbuses, things leaning
every-so-slightly into each
other's tinted glow, making finally a

gigantic ring of light with
everything in it in the

fixed material world, but everything constantly
leaving and entering it, a visible

reflection in space of rings around the moon on one of those
mysterious clear nights when the
whole fluffy sky seems to be airily centralized around a

luminous point!

Down here in my
little room, thinking human thoughts of being
a person on a planet with its
moon *"up there"* in a
certain picturesque display, not

catching the
cold lifeless wind blowing across

moon-dust, kicking some
    up, not much, but
a few stray gray
    grains or two, dry
crack in the
lunar loneliness, echo but

no reply, I

sit here having these
pictures, Blake figures, pale
yellow as moonlight, slinkily

stretched to
    prophetic extensions of them-
        selves, also occasionally

blowing very white transparent
trumpets, leaning in

amazed arcs and
blowing right into our
consciousness some

otherworldly reveille, Blake was

so concerned with

waking up, like a
snoring body sitting up suddenly enough for the
factory walls built around it in the

night to
crack into dust, each
note floating
        off into
            eternity, high pure

note of trumpet in that
call, chimney-stacks and
        brothels,
our usual Western ways, the economic
pleasures of
White Supremacy! Precision

parts and
casual sex. *Immorality Imports!*

Natives line up at
        docks for their
            dose! Trading in their
    sweet brown skins and
ancient fragrances for a
suit of stripes and some
        supermarket chains where
            everything's made in
Taiwan. I've

been to African marketplaces invaded by the
West and Russia and China, and
though each month Nigerians get malaria,
and there is a tree whose brewed bark
completely offsets its effects, now they

can't remember which one it is.
The drugstore does the job for them:
Chloroquin, at 14 Naira a bottle,
made from that very same tree-bark, processed and
bottled in England, sold back to Africans by
    British Pharmaceuticals,

the natives lining up at the
local drugstore doing a
   brisk business.

2

*No, no! This isn't
right,* not

malaria – *melody!* Trumpet of

glass held at a
certain angle to catch along its

top side galaxies, along its

bottom side cityscapes, horizon lines at

night like the ones that go round the
edge of a planetarium, sleepy, twinkling,
and as I put it to my lips

it floats further upward, or

I float, and the

music comes through from
elsewhere, not merely

making out the notes we've
all heard before, re-
jumbling car-horns and
dawn-birds, blue jays and
jazz, but

from Elsewhere, syncopated

scoops of
      down-trills and
scales as if the pageant of
sky's aurora borealis were
      translated into

sound.
Totem poles actually talking! Ice bridges singing
      arias across glaciers, snowflakes
            whistling as they fall! The ocean actually

getting up on its knees and finally
saying what it's been trying to
say all this time, in its
wish-wash of exuberant
tides, or we could actually

hear the speech of old Sequoias, eloquent

interlocutors of interglacial
happenings, and they could

hauntingly recreate the primordial
scene. Rivers already

    sing, creeks gossip, even
      shy rocks sitting under
    glitter of watery
        surfaces hum to
      themselves.

Open up our earthly pores to
sound-showers, open up our

ears clogged with clay for
centuries, but each set a set of

perfect flute-pipes cut from
original bamboo stalks blowing ethereal
melodies already on

otherworldly shores,
holes pierced at perfect intervals to hear

earth' s
delirious

tune!

3

I'd like the
poem to open up the way a

pure trumpet note opens up
blue-silver space where

before there was
textured obscurity, like a

ski-slope of glass that goes
upward or

outward evenly in
unlimited extension, or

limited by breath, as long as
the breath expands, so that

you don't have to read
words on a page or even hear

that earthy human vocal sound made up of
hums and growls and

cutting *s's* popping
p's or *t's* that

slice off
thought, though there's something

rich in
r's, treasure of

polished opals, dark rounded
jewels laid on velvet, and the

vowels are always beautiful, soothing,
inviting, why

Rimbaud liked them
so, saw real colors flying

out of them, pictures
suspended in their open-air theatres of

sound, but I would have a
note, a single

note, and as it grows
thinner the poem's particular

landscape would unroll, and you would be
in it the way you've been in the

countryside, in the
middle of a field, burrs on your

socks, your shirt smelling of
sweat and pollen, far distant

cow-bells, soft clatter of bicycle, or the

sound across the valley of someone

pulling nails out of wood with a
hammer, woodpecker in a tree, the

green smell of
growth, buzzing right in your ear, sound of

grasses blowing,
rot-smell of logs or leaves, heat vaguely

oppressive, making you
sleepy, although you're

awake, eyes trying to get
meaning out of scanning the skyline, the

mountainous horizon, dry
California hills, fine powdery

dirt in the
wind,

the poem opening up the way
this has opened up

enveloping you, carrying you
on its rhythms like muscular

outriggers going oceanward, catching the
veiled themes of wonder and

how it vibrates the catalog of the universe into a
visual picture, transparent as

glass, finally a
sound, high-pitched and pure, but with a

low rumble implied,
wordless chute out past distractions onto

fields of Divine labor where the heart is
halved and put

back again
whole, each

valve oiled

song.

4/7

WE CAN'T STOP SINGING

We can't stop singing – if we do
telephone poles in this world would
    fall down. Crickets under
hedges or in doorways would look back with those
regal, sad, black-button eyes then
pack up their back legs and
        saunter off. A certain

ringing of the human presence bounces off
walls and mountains, just as the

Prophet David sang and the
mountains echoed and angels echoed back the
mountains, grass blades made
spontaneous harps, even

stones like tympanis lined up with their
throaty booms, because

somewhere in the human heart caught fire or
suddenly expanded a hundred times its size
and took in distant palaces and vistas never-before-seen,
    never-before-heard –

crunch of naked foot on white beach sand
in Pacific Isle, breezes making
bamboo hum dry crackles –

and long, slow insect buzz is drone to these ragas!

When the
    throat opens
        doors open,

steps appear down which
   white-clad figures carrying exotic trays of fruit
      steaming in a silver entwining of
atmospheres approach and
absorb our inspirations into
    delectable gamelans.

Our place in nature is
singing. In this we exceed the
      inarticulate crocodile.
Lying flat, just eyes above the surface of that
black water, what does he
    sing? Snapping of plated
jaws, that's all.

Not us. Out come
pearls. And
what's in the
heart is their
velvet-lined
gestation place.

Deep in the
center of its
own sea.

                                       4/14

THERE'S A SUNSET OUT THERE

There's a sunset out there that could
    only be portrayed musically,
some gloriously outfurling
    chord on some
resonant piano, cellos and
    violins underneath with an
    expansive throb, triangles and
      celestas tinkling mightily,
  all of it
    incredibly
      clear in the
ear, to somehow capture the

golden-pink majesty of all-along-the-horizon-of-the-
city this kind of watercolor
  melting of shadings into the
    gun-gray sky, with
      black streaks and light streaks, all of it
turning somber as
night comes on, catching the
    hearts of the
citizens scurrying home, or coming home with
  supper groceries, or
sitting in their
oak-panelled rooms with a
single incense smoke-strand
  making knots in the
    air, untying then
dying away,

or the moisture in the
        throat of the
one in that room, caught in mid-
swallow while utter
        clarity invades his
            heart, opens
titanic
tunnels of light in his
thoughts, dispels thought
        for even a
second that seems like
never, held up in the
            air like a
diamond drop of spittle on the glinting
        tip of a
dark needle, as the
        room itself
            darkens, and the
crisp silence silkens into a

blank brocade, tiny
threads of clicking
noises of motionlessness
standing still from its
center, letting facets of
minute movements and great
silences make
        squeaking
    wedges in the

air, he sits, the

room sits with him, the room
sits inside him, he is

naked on a
hilltop with the whole

cityscape in-
    side him, lights of
cars on their
    way home, darkness
painting the
tops of ocean
    waves which
incandesce as they
pour over, he

sits facing space the way bright
day comes out of
night, clouds above the

sunset look like lead, the
sun is

down,
his

heart is

still.

4/15

SINGLE BIRD

Salut a Lui chaque fois
Que chante le coq gaulois
　　　　— Arthur Rimbaud

Single bird on a
　　　hilltop of blue ice,
preposterous vision! Sing your

　　　heart out! Out of the

daily walking around, wanting the choppy
　　　ocean waves of
　　　　　passionate
　　　　　　　discourse to
carry me away on
　　　golden crests,

now, at night, surrounded by
street sounds, is the heart this
　　　　single bird like a
nocturnal
　　　rooster crowing the
　　　　　Creator's praise alone under an
upside-down barn rooftop imagined sticking
　　　　out of a
　　　　　　cloud?

Or is it a peacock of
self-involvement on the
　　　tip of a

sphere spreading its
        splendor in
ocular taillights, only
shrieking? Or could it be a

snowy egret, the
great blue heron standing still, or

the lyrebird out of its
tropical element,

bowerbird arranging bits of
    coral, shell and
        Coca-cola bottle caps in intriguing
patterns for its
        paramour to be
            attracted to,

single bird, above all,
on a peak of blue ice, to
    accentuate its
singleness, being my

being at night alone after longing for
praise-oceans to
    sway me into
  spectacular
        Presence,

reflections of His
sunlight everywhere

mingling in lunar outline on wave-tops

as the song is sung

on an
ice-peak in

Reality where

I don't exist.

Just

sound.

                                                    4/22

IF I WERE TO GO TO AN ISLAND

If I were to go to an island it would be
ringed around with pink flamingos,
heat would boil up through banyans,

natives, in the
    majority, would have a
language like sing-song they would
    yodel with flashing teeth, there'd be an

impeccable tropicalness, a clean
torrid severity, languor in the way

giant plants would effloresce
    everywhere swishing
        back and forth constantly,
turquoise waters casting
mirror-like flashes against half-submerged
    tree trunks, roots like
feet of prehistoric mammoths gone
deep into mud and just
        staying there, vapors of many
colors twining and intertwining like
braids on a petulant girl-child chattering
incessantly to herself in a
        bedroom mirror,

I'm transported into this Latin latticework of
leafy green and gold against a

sea of nothing that's not natural, there'd be

smells of pungent growth and rot,
    rot at the same rate as birth taking
everything away in
        pungent bits, including

our selves, smells and
    torrid sights,
medleys of sound indescribable except with a
background of muted marimbas,

sea-waves make the rhythmic sizzle behind it all
as its mumbling melodies weave
trances come right out of
tree-bark and up from stones.

Something about
water, moisture alone
        musical, hot
mist hanging between
trees – and we haven't even mentioned
        the birds and animals!

Or down at the
nearsighted level, *insects*, Baroque
royalty in the tropics, definitely
extraterrestrial, always traveling
    incognito! Creeping in so
        trying-to-be-anonymous, but
so completely eccentric in the way

Allah's created them with long
    waggling feelers, or
bizarre pointed snouts and
    hamster eyes on
sleek green bodies!

Tropical variety endless, each
natural niche filled, there's

completeness to the
texture of the
tapestry,

there's
sunlight on the
water you can

walk on, there's a
flute from the
heart of the

forest that

calls your name!

4/29

THE LAST DAY

1

It's said the Last Day's heralded
by a Cry, high-pitched
dissolver of matter at all
    altitudes, cuts

right through to the
bottom of the sea, high as the
highest icy peak of the Alps,
splits the whole

universe into
fuzz-balls, power of

sound, or sound the

scrape of something so huge, cat-gut bow scraped
slowly along the edge of the
gong of creation to send

shivers through matter from which it
    never recovers
with afterwards nothing but a long dull stretch of
soundlessness and only a

single dust-dot floating at an
angle through space, or a

holding of breath?

Do we make such a cry at the
moment of death, high-pitched in its
secret domain, wheeze of the

old geezer breathing his last on his death-bed, but enough to
    slice down through the
molecules of our lives, or is it just a

guttural slice of silence suddenly unloosed in

a flight of air out the
    body into
        bodiless space?

What was the sound of the Big Bang, something so singly
deafening that it's
taken this long to define into

lark arcing gently over open field, pine-needles hissing on a hilltop,
love-language passing through the lips of the
        lovely beloved,

or Mexican Corrida music right now come bursting over our
        fence at,
    God! Midnight!
All sonorous threads branching out from

Original Roar, no
bull bellowing, no lion enraged could

perform, at the
    peak of its
       ecstatic
fearsomeness, no railroad screaming through a
tunnel in Magnetic Mountain could come close
to the sound that set all things in motion,
blowing individual tones out in
          space like
  hairs floating out in the
       air of the
    loved one's head, gold lights going
         white from the
            glare, each

murmur being the mouth in this sphere at this
time from that
crescendo before time began which had no
mouth but was

     pure sound!

Tiny pen-scratch to write this, branch rubbing my
window-pane, wind in the

banana-tree out front,
    drunk Mexican
voices of fiesta next door also part of that
ubiquitous cosmic growl that will

end in one shout that flattens

everything everywhere suddenly

for all time

forever!

2

Seated on the floor before the
book *"Galaxies,"* seeing the

galaxies in glossy colored pictures on the page

I can't imagine them as silent,

there has to be a concordance of
   sound, chords in
     round swirls like the
       light and particles of these
gargantuan jelly-fish bodies themselves
     hanging in

deep space, upright at their
special angle and
absolutely suspended in their
own atmospheres, making

such unique noise, *but what is it?* Is it

gravelly and twittering at the

same time, like

sizzle of sand as wind
picks it up and heaves it in
    sheets across space like some

cosmic bereavement, mournful and
endlessly sifting, the sound of

honeybees in their
hives, sizzling
buzz of molecular
activity,

or turn the heavy pages to
Galaxy M33, *"A member of the*
    Local Group located near the
    Andromeda Galaxy, presents a
    relatively open face to
    our galaxy," like

elements bubbling up in liquid, froth from
air itself breathing, non-cohesive, disjunct spots of
nebulae, bits aswirl, totally

silent to
themselves, but I can't imagine them

silent, they sit

in all their glittery glory

silent on the
page, in my

room at night in the

same exact space they
actually exist in, and there's certainly

no silence here!

Everything but what is Allah has
noise, and Allah sends us His

Names and Attributes in the noise-filled
world of our senses, He is their

Origin, creation itself His

loudspeaker, the
Prophet himself Allah's
transmitter in earth-space, we with our
   limited ears, walking
   two-legged radios
     tuning in,

ghetto-blasters on
legs, along wild worldly
alleyways, turning our

knobs back and forth to pinpoint that

galactic music

    that is not
        quite sound but at the same time is

not at all

silent.

3

What a mystery it is, riding along in the
   cave of the car, the
mechanical cavernous streamlined box on wheels
that *is* a car, gliding through
    space with all the
piston and cast-iron
upheavals exploding *sotto voce* inside the hood, and
our two children in the back seat,
girl age six, boy age ten, talking, arguing,
   expressing their
      private intensities, trying to

explain something in rudimentary detail using an
    incomplete vocabulary from their
      perfect but
          immature perspective, the

car filling up with their words and the
sounds of their voices, young

brooks,
        fluid dimension of
pristine
    natural things, like
        small animals, a certain
squeakiness to their
                sound, a small
                furriness filling the
car, poignant even in
    grumpiness, which is
    (at their ages) often,

fights, then a
sudden revelation, excitement, they are

so themselves, I driving along with the
Drive-In movie-screen of my
    own thoughts filling with
method actor superstars, each so
preoccupied and sincere, suddenly these

sharp voices from the back seat like the
zinging of arrows come straight at us, their
mother and I, with such
thought-shattering simplicity, and such

sound, in moving
    space, so
suspended in the
        automobile's mobile atmosphere, as if

plucked from the surface of the
planet to connect with other

slightly disembodied
        sounds, like

fledglings squawking in their
        nests, budding
Madame Curies or
Carl Jungs actually having a
totally profound discovery for
        themselves, they

hand over in words to us their
own individualities,

they are *not* us, but
part of us, we have so many

references in common, it all

starts from
this, small

family in a
car,

talking!

4

In the silent space between
dream and waking
our body is in one place and
gets up in another with no
        scraping.

Suddenly we aren't where we *weren't,*
sit up in a room in the dark with the
    ordinary sounds of
        three dimensions
rushing in. No

throb of piano-board strings being
struck, resonant fellows in
    sympathy all down the
        line to the
        high register, where before there were

voices, an airy
melodious crackle, even
music itself, or its
    sheen, insistent drumming, maybe our own
heartbeats in our ears, the

fulsome blood going
    round in our
heads, a
rhythm at least, maybe
        jogging those delirious

pictures along, our
pulse-like sprockets to
   guide the
      picture-ribbon
through,

then we wake in the room and it's
gone, the actual battery-run
quartz alarm-clock next to us on the bedside table
all the heart-throb we know now

ticking minutes along in this
other space where the

febrile argument of that
other world, the connected

animated full-color hauntingly
real story-line, accompanied by a

rush of good sound and its everlasting
echoes

is gone.

5

I get up the second night,

the same thing happens,

the same sensation,

(I'm one of those
get-up-once-in-the-night-to-pee
people),

a sudden cessation of sound, cut
off from the

dream, sitting up in the
aftermath like in the

sudden silence
just after loud

music stops.

5/2 – 10

PART 2

GLINTING TIP OF BIRD-BEAK

for Malika

Glinting tip of bird-beak in the dark
arcing at an angle into the murk of
    an imagined rain forest during
  love-making, surrounding what

used to be the bedroom with miles of
  trees in all directions, we're
    in the middle, being
bodily, hoots and

hyena-bird's laughter reverberating mockingly through the
trees that are
    actually nothing multiplying within the
      four walls of our
  room, then

water-gush (it's on the
    cassette-tape), water-glisten
      for environmental
listening, we're

drowned in natural
sound as if under

mulch in a colony of friendly
buzzes, there are very gold

sunlight-shafts splitting up and
beaming down through the
forested thickness, there are

such growths entwining us that in the
light (the lights are out) we would be just

faces and shoulders completely engulfed in
    vines, tendrils completely em-
        broidering our
bodies, the

sweat-beads of our love feeding their
thirsty green molecules, but in the

darkness that is
endlessly velvety and endlessly deep, we are

bodiless sensations entwined in root-and-vine outlines
existing almost as if suspended in the
air rather than
    part of the
      earth because we are

lying so close together on the bed and there are no
dimensions or limits to our

hearing, senses inter-
    mingle, that

distant bird-shriek becomes part of the

generalized purple or

far-off chartreuse, there are only

jeweled presences here, and we are

embedded among them,
breathing on our
            own.

Worlds light up from time to time just past the
        thickets, then there is
            cool darkness again, then

more worlds light up, in slow

rotation. We are

here, in a pivotal leaf, they are at the

edges, passing across our edges like

        serrated gears, their

movement in
proportional slow-

motion to our
stillness,

migrations have

stopped here to
rest, boastful plumage is
all in potential, nothing's
        unfurled or needing to be
            displayed, it is

O.K. to be quiet in the
dark, twitterings of

underbrush birds don't even

cancel the dark, nor the
        silence, there is

simply continuum, high up, containing even the

lowest live encroachments, the

sleepiest mud-slurp where pink and whitish
        worms make their way to a
deeper dark.

It's O.K. to be
        quiet in the

dark.

5/12

THE NATURAL SHAPE OF MAN

The natural shape of man is worship.
Until we fully inhabit that shape
we are not truly human.

And there is space for right or
wrong worship, connection with
Source or self-defeat, at one with the

No-Image of Divine Tremendous Love
or enwrapped at the wooden feet of false idols in
drafty temples on the Upper Nile, silver

winds to choke us as we try to
breathe, awaiting those lapis lazuli lips to
open and speak!

The natural mode of man is search.
Else why have we been
born on two three-dimensional legs and

restless, having to set out from our
mothers with our father's blessing, going where
no one has ever gone before, or rather

where *we* haven't gone before, melting
invisibly into the Adamic caravan that
weaves all the way back to

first man and woman who ever

cast a glance around them and
wondered where they were and who their

Originator, Who their
predecessor, Who *created* them out of the
glistening air that fills with

sunlight in the morning and casts out its
velvets of stars at night across the
top of our world. Eyes that look, both

out and in, at each
other.

That stepping off into
what it is to be
human, and then to

make choices based on the heart's bent, leaning on
whispers or statements in our
blood, atoms get up on their legs and

direct us in angelic formation to take
this or that road, to love
this or that creature or

lack of creature, mistakenly
worshipping our own
bodily shapes as they are or could

be, too soon

wrinkling out of
sight, losing that physical

elasticity that
attracted those
women to the

face of Joseph, toward a
beauty that was
deeper, or we

worship what we are
not, *wrong turn*, we wake up
dissatisfied with who we

see stretched out before us from our eyes to the
tips of our feet, and want to be
elsewhere and *other*,

or we set out within the delirious
orbit of our own awakening
to dismantle the educated response, the

obsession to concretize and fix reality into
non-fleeting shapes instead of
throwing it like a cloud-ball at a

single divine target, ourselves

that shooting-gallery, until
we strike One! All failures

fall away, the

long shadow covers us, brown
darkness descends, a small
yellow glow ignites within it

to illuminate our
faces, and we are
alone with The Alone,

and at one with The

One Who doesn't

multiply but whose

many Presences coalesce

around us to

shiver us

past our bones.

5/14

THE PERFECT ORCHESTRA

1

The perfect orchestra:

Niagara Falls as string section
providing constant undercurrent and
sizzle, tone, total wrap-around
    continuum, mist of
noise always near but dimensionally non-
        locatable in space –

for horns:
the city of London, downtown, say, Oxford Street at
4:00 p.m., buses honking, taxis, the
    sing-song of sirens cutting
      through it all on their
        way to
  disaster, the tone of it abruptly
      changing as it
    passes, intelligent
texture of almost
vocal horn-sounds, in tinny
  dialogue and un-
      muffled modulations, stitching our
 up-tight urban life together at
    seams we couldn't
   possibly let go in
     silence, or else
antlers and tops of fir trees would

appear where
    shop-fronts are, and all our
hard-won victory over nature would be lost —

for flutes:
old bones, say,
elephant bones from their
cemeteries in solitude, or the tiny inconspicuous
bones of hummingbirds just before they
        dissolve entirely
            away, or the
fragile sheaths of
fingernail-like bone-material that's
        wrapped around
pin-feathers just before they open out in
display, or
the underground network of
pipelines and
    sewers in the world linked up and made to
chant their inhuman groans —

for triangles:
icicles, the high-pitched ping of frozen water from
Siberian eaves, cracked off just before the
    concert and tapped on the
        edge of a cave, a lost cave somewhere in, say,
the hills of Mongolia, also of
ice, also of high-pitched
        brittle ping, enough to set
caribou pricking their ears and rolling those
great dark eyes like illumined

marbles back in their
    sockets to
  see what was
    there –

for a chorus:
the three billion human souls suffering
hurt, or displacement, or starvation, torture or
   unyielding injustice somewhere, getting
together to join
voices into
one voice, which makes the
single sound of the
    human heart in one
  crescendo, like the roar of
   a single
    heartbeat, and if we can do
nothing to change things from where we sit at least we would
go to our graves with the
   haunting poignant sound
    of humankind heard for once above the
small talk of our too small
lives on earth –

for piano:
the entire animal kingdom, alligator ripple-spine,
glockenspiel-like bird-clucks, trills of
   forest-birds, cackle of
    jays, flap of
seal-flippers, yell of
  sea-lions –

for brass section:
light-rays from clouds, high
altitude lightning-bolts, laser-beams bounced
   off the moon, long clear notes extending
      past our atmosphere –

for harp:
the sound of wind through vines
    hanging down in
       rainforests, their
tips touching the surface of
      swamp waters as they
slowly trickle past –

for drums, tympani, wood-blocks, snares:
the dry earth itself in its deepest eruptions,
earthquakian, volcanic, seismographic,
shaken loose at last, its
       voice seeking relief, its
voice without tempo, always
    breaking out of
      rhythmic regularity with
        inspired syncopation, dis-
rupting the
   norms, now
waltz-time, now
   elegiac,
    lyrical, then
      tragic, earth's booming
swivel on its
axis in the

auditorium of
        space,

where a crowd of listeners listens, who are the
Sound-Maker Himself, Allah alone

listening to Himself, in the single

purity of His Face!

2

Having assembled the orchestra we stand up
and are washed away by water, hand raised with a
baton of air we are engulfed by air and swept into
anywhere, arching forward to lean into the

about-to-be articulated
sound coming out of the round void, the lovely
void like the bell of a flower devours us
whole, swallows us down and plants us

deep in the soil of pure sound, having
envisioned the orchestra behind the
façade of my four walls, we are melted away
back into sound as the ground of our

being in all its teeming variety, all the way to
night-heron honk on Bolinas Lagoon long ago
as they sailed out over the water to begin their

nightly prowl.

Is there a Chinese orchestra in a smoky
basement in Canton right now with all their
fragile instruments, reeds and strings and
paper-dry skin pulled taut over gourd-bowl
sounding bells, tuning up with the

music of natural dissonance, like their
language itself, sing-song and
pliable, peaking in a
high-pitch before

sliding down the scale, right
now as I write this about to begin their
concert of traditional tunes, the
Snow-goose Song, or the First Tap of Spring
on the Window-pane-like Lake Surface!

All the gorgeous vast and incomparable
sweep of nature itself shrunk down to a
few flutes and quavering strings, yet

powerful as

a phenomenon, translated into notes by

touch or

breath.

3

Sitting in a back garden full of plants,
they make no sound.

Rustling of breeze through leaves, but
nothing they say that we can

hear on their
own. A ninety-two year old woman talks about

death, her
upcoming one, her

sister who died of cancer,
and the plants sit around in their pots keeping quiet

as her words float around like a
dry watering can, drifting

slightly reedy words like kind
nutrition on her

leafy darlings, as she
sits in a

chair in a
straw hat, her

gnarled hands
tossing on her

knees.
She can't remember who was

President when she was
born, the

rush of excitement about life is
gone, the

plants are silent yet she and they are
vaguely the same, they sit so

still and patient in their pots, awaiting their
fate.

4

Then there's the body as orchestra,
        basking in its own pure
                beauty, starting from the

drum-pads of the feet on asphalt, on hard-packed
dirt, the shuffle and beat, on

    sand, the softer swish, flesh-pads brushing
            jostling grains, or the

longer trombone slides of the legs,
scissoring motions, propulsion ahead by the
        slide's long extension, floating us

along on loping undertones as we
   turn our eyes slyly right and
       left at the
   interiorized
      world as we go, then there is the

cello-section of the
hips, the pelvic solar plexus, deeper and
mellower in tone, reaching sustained low

registers in tumultuous or
harmonious chords, suns rise from there
either blackened or burnished by the
   light of the
      skies they rise through, and higher up

the stomach, nervous flutes and gastric clarinets,
bowels of bassoons, the gurgle of saxophones,

then higher to the heart, whose music is
most mysterious, most full, most
   breakable, most pure, the violins in
unison, poignant, shrill, reaching

unbearable heights of longing and delight,
loquacious melodies, springing

suddenly from gloom, or the long

drone tones, as of bees inside their hives, in their
angelic hierarchies, each

pumping honey through their
    pipes,

then up to the throat, choruses and solo voices,
bassos and sopranos, the history of the
human voice from aborigine to now, burst

forth, the glory of song! Nothing sounds quite

like it, it fills
    canyons and
        cathedrals
           equally!
Heard from a distance,

such intimacy, such
    recognition! The human
voice can go anywhere! Its first notes
are search, its last notes
        love.

Then to the piccolos of the eyes, the flash and
    glint of whistling
      clarity, cymbals and
        bells, each
ringing with
    brightness. Then the

piano of intellect, capable of reason, as well as

flight from reason, clusters of

dissonance, as well as

a few perfect notes depressed at
    one touch, making

just the hint of eternity wink out from
the echo, or the

dazzling pyrotechnic runs up and down the
    scale, missing almost

none of the
keys in the
process, to a final chord so

comprehensive it forms a

total door of sound the flesh body walks through to

silence.

5/22

THE INITIAL CREATIONAL GESTURE

1

The initial creational gesture was the vocalized word: *Be!*
Big Bang is one name for it, in our
    myopic history, looking at drifting
      debris and deducing the
light of the
impact at the beginning, failing to see how that
moment continues its impact at this
moment on all
    fronts, *collapsible*

    creation! This moment

kissing that moment in a perfect
circle
rolling on these hills. Articulate

Igniter, *"Be!"* standing in

space like the breath-hole of a soap-bubble about to
    float free.

Coasting over our heads into pale blue sky
    glinting reflections of
      skyscrapers which are
        actually coming
down from the
    sky upside-down to

populate our
    brittle imaginations with
        spike-tops and
forty floors of plate glass.

Are we standing on the earth on our two feet
with yellow clouds wrapping our
heads in hot towels, craning to hear

that first word sounding from a peak of pure silver
past all toxic distractions? I mean

hear that word spoken by its Speaker, I

mean lean forward to catch its
    intonations, actually make a
move like a
   movement in the
      heart to hear it

for it is

actually being spoken here!

2

Common sounds of room and house
running up and down domestic scales, voice
of mother scolding daughter with
huskier tone than usual, poignant

voice of daughter's reply, higher, weaker than
usual, using a warble to achieve the
desired effect of hurt pride and momentary
    self-image wobble,

sound of street outside, some homemade go-cart wheels
hacking at the sidewalk as if they were square,

sound of space itself, space the
   city sits in all the way
      to the sea, a

glisten in the ear —

echoes along rampart walls, that huge domed
room in Granada's Alhambra
architecturally designed so when you
lean against one of the concrete ribs that
   lead up to the arched roof and whisper
it can be heard as clear as normal speech by
someone all the way across the room putting their ear
against an opposite rib, or

voices of dry wind whistling across Teotihuacan
pyramid square, where only
tourists and ants wobble in the sun, dry

as dust, you can

almost hear ancient Toltec voices telling tales
no hieroglyphs can adequately

explain!

3

We see out past the particular ledge set up with its
iron dolls and rusted books in front of watery windows that
look only one way, they are so
thin that some worlds won't fit inside their
    thicknesses, we actually

look out past crowding and unforested
imaginary avenues that lead straight out to a
common center, we look out and out

in somewhat straight lines past even that
imagined focal point, suddenly there are

white domed houses around us sitting in front of sand-dunes,
the dunes change shape but the houses remain the same, the
inhabitants change and are born and die with the
dazzling dunes but the
walls and doors of the houses remain with their
    cheerful smiles of whiteness looking out on the
        shifting dunes, we look past even these
fascinating and lively fictions, past flatness and tallness,
roundness or squareness, then when we've looked past
them we go on to look past

empty space. There are skies so
empty a single voice can be heard

echoing in them, fleecy edges of

fluffy whiteness around pellucid blue only gives the
voice's echo a shiver like audible lace, there are

beams crisscrossing in that empty space to make
nets of silence, and sound-waves

bounce back to life when they
land in their mesh, but we look past even

this to where eyes give out, white-washed walls of
nothing at all framing visual regions fall away

and there is a sigh of their falling like old Hunza ladies'
voices in mountains where the
marvelous balance of nature lets people live to be over
    a hundred years old, until they've

finally had enough and want to die, we stop

seeing, we stop projecting pictures past where pictures cannot go,
there is suddenly no describable world here, we are
surrounded by pure *surroundingness*, or we are

around ourselves in what surrounds us, but

one sounded note of immaterial nature beams toward us,
like a down-turned fountain its celestial spray splashes
around us in the
swiftest and sweetest

tones, and the

white light in our blood makes a parallel rising tone,
and there is

one braided tone resulting.

4

In the natural scheme of things: An oriole singing
   as only an oriole can, its sound
pointing back to the
      origin of its song – I have to add

clock-tick and ringing in the
ear, because that's what I
hear here at 3:00 a.m., having

woken up with those
first lines about the
   bird in my head, after
taking a pee I
   come back to
write it down and
      add on, thinking, *"not just a
loose catalog starting with the
oriole and trying to somehow get
everything else in the
universe into it,"* with the idea again

and again that its
sound points back to the
origin of its song and is, in its

openly joyful noise, the

totally exact reverberation of that
initial *"Be!"* of creation

articulated by Allah to get

every

being going.

5/22 – 6/1

SITTING AS WE ARE

Sitting as we are on the precise
needle-tip of space/time existence,
silver glinting in the
light of the beginning as well as the
    end of time (legs dangling ever so
loosely over the edge), and violet clouds from
high altitudes massively moving like dreaming
bison through our heads, ears cocked to hear

bell-sound or bugle-call, we find ourselves

sonically and radiantly at the
apex cross-hairs of everything that
exists and everything that ever
    existed, as well, dear
created beings, peach-fuzz-cheek
magnets of existences so
exotic as to be
indescribable, drawn to you
just by your having been born!

We don't have to do
anything, make no effort to have
rainbows complete their arcs to
    die in our hair,
ghosts of fences torn down long ago to
make thrill-itches along our
scapulae, or the

dance of seasons in
Beethovianic regalia
leave tracks in our
bodies, sinuses, livers, the
identifiable pad-swirls of our
antenna-like
    fingertips.

We are grooves of records the needle fits so
   snugly into to make
     sound emerge around which our
amorphous swoon into amazement takes on
bodily form, and we

walk away like someone whose winning ticket has
just been announced, to have
   suddenly attached to our
persons silver-white stallions from Greek
mythology, ancient sistrums
chang-changing delicately in
     lustrous blue air.

O Lord of our heartbeats, hidden Lord whose
Face is in evidence but Who can't be
   described, each possible description leaves
lips in flame where their
     words took flight,

they circle like stones in tide pools, reflecting only
light from an above light-source, circulating
as dumbly as

that which waits to be wholly animated from Elsewhere,
and when that
    animation comes great white
        stripes of light in
barber-pole fashion

wrap themselves up around the

Words' *ascendancies!*

                                        6/12

THE BOOK IS EVERYWHERE

1

The Book is everywhere
from which we pluck these roses,

its pages are air
turning one at a time.

Faces emerge speaking comprehensible phrases
then fold back into something

closing, turning away toward a
source beyond us,

elephants balancing on lily pads in silver water
inside a spoon held up

almost to our lips, our eyes
watching shadow-shows of exaggerated gestures

gyrate perpetual motion on a white screen while
an invisible narrator in high-pitched

sing-song actually
relates events in a

chronological sequence that ends up having
everything to do with our

lives, which are sharply profiled
also circulating in shadow!

Our clear-cut anonymous lives move like
blood through space being pumped by sidereal

presences. We float past
faces of planets,

luminosities of galaxies lying on their sides like
overblown roses on black teak

tables of outer space, scarlet
petals drifting –

the fragrance of those
roses reaches our nostrils

and we burst into song!

Plucking the archetypes from
that Book that lets verbalized

breath flow out from its
cloud-shaped pages

passing through
white walls of space

like bursts of gray light, then
white, like sailing panes of

glass, like
page-shaped

clouds.

2

A hoof hits turf, a buzz
crosses a pool, shadow zigzagging beneath it, a

light comes on in a forest
but no one's there, a chattering of

selves in the shelves of the trees, birds with
necks like complicated

plumbing, whose
cries crisscross space with

hyena-laughter, echoing
back again as

angel's song.
Night falls and

faces grow silent, day
comes and dew-damp

noses begin to
twitch,

ants like threads sewing up seams in the earth
make their straight-line march to

strategic destinations, wind
blows bringing pollen,

trees shift slightly in their
roots, waters

imperiously rush down a sheer
stairway of rocks, and these are the

transparent pages of the Book that turn through our
lungs and sensitive organs even while we

sleep! Cells from one
creature to the next set up

telephonic communication
24 hours a day.

Our corpuscles make long distance calls to the
dolphins and get

Wagnerian replies. There are
lives to be saved. Each creature looks after its own.

And then after each other's!
No shadow crosses the face of a

creature but that its

angle reveals an

expression so pure and
poignant

everything on its
way somewhere stops

still in its tracks for a second in the air to
behold itself and the

rapture of its
natural beauty!

Silver braids of
steaming light rise straight up above

normal grottos.
Dragonflies skim backwards.

Deer families come down
one by one, very

cautious-paced, nostrils like
radar stations, to stand by

flowing streams and bend
sleek necks to their
sizzlings.

Our consciousness in imagination

goes deep into the forest from our

city beds and looks around with the great
light it's got, and

sees these things! How can we not
notice the barely visible

twitches and tiny
breaths from

where we are?
Things under ferns, behind logs, floating down-

stream in
early morning

sunlight?
Our bodies also flat inside the

pressed paper of the Book's
turning pages stood

up at the side of the
forest-pool to look

out on the
abundance that

fans together here!
And this is the Book that sees us and that

we see, we reach
way down into it to bring up these

blazing
texts covered with larvae and

cocoon-shells, cobwebs and
the gummy substances of life that

bursts from a
sexual center to

throb with the
tone of one

harp string plucked like a
note of gold

above
dark water.

3

The Book has death in it,
and life. As soon as you
    strike a match
        orange flame flares up, the
wood turns black and it
    starts dying. Hedges run along

fields all the
    way to the sea. Life thrives
        inside them.
Fields are
    plowed, mouse-dens and
gopher-holes destroyed, while the

hedge life buzzes along as
before. A fly in my

lamp distracts me as I
    write this, seeing the
English countryside in my
    mind from my
bed in Santa Barbara,

far and near become joined in alchemical marriage,
life meets death halfway and

a blue door is opened in glacial façade and
a yellow light can be
    seen in it
toward which
    we turn.

The Book has life in it,
and death. A black rectangle with
    silver edging
glides down between
    buildings in the
air for us to

walk through. Before there was

no thought of our dying, *ever!* We'd get
older and more wrinkled, wiser and more
bent, more smiling and forgetful, loving our
grandchildren to death, but never

really dying ourselves, but when we

walk through that black rectangle, of near-
miss, or premonition, or being

witness to death's actual glass harpsichord, and
walk free of death's damp sheets in a
        hot summer in Pennsylvania

and find ourselves in a garden with
white picket fence in which there is a
lion as well as a dairy-cow, a
        waterfall as well as a
                brick house, a
contract beyond the grave as well as an
entire opera to our mortality, then

envelopes become four-dimensional, hair becomes
five, speech becomes six,
the seven-dimensional glance transcends them
        all, and arrives at
primordial concentration, all
        space and time
                enfolded in its

sphere,

light like out-of-focus snowflakes of perfect formation
radiates into the silhouettes we
      recognize coming toward us as
            matter, we
talk with seeming
      emptiness and get
            comprehensible reply,

hooves of distant horsemen can be heard
receding, the

scrunch of the present moment underfoot

arriving.

The Book has
death in it, and life,

life in it, and death —

A black

doorway fills with

light and

ignites the shapes

we file through.

4

*"Did their winds tell thee where they rested
at noontide?" She said, "Yes, they rested
    at Dhat al-Ajra'
Where the white tents are radiant with
those rising suns within."*
— Shaykh Ibn al-'Arabi
(Tarjuman al-Ashwaq XXIV)

I could hear the steady
        shhhh of the
    wind through the huge oak tree in back
as I took a past-midnight shower
        after love-making,
water washing down my body as
wind whooshes through branches and
    rattles the corrugated
            tin on the
        car-port, and saw in my

mind a globe that is the earth in a space that is the
Universe with atmospheric turgidity rushing in
amorphous clumps of cloud around the
sphere we're on, brushing it

up as you would the
nap of a woolen coat, but with

wind-brushes, scattering
tree-leaves in swirling directions, hair on our
heads, hats down

streets, wind from stars maybe

reaching us all the way down
here from their
    outermost reaches, and I

wondered if winds actually die, or only
pass and move on, perpetually motioning in
    perpetual motion, to
        fold and delve back into the
galactic ocean and then

circle round again, and if they are the

same winds from the same active air of a
billion years ago, did they

graze the cheeks of Neanderthals, our close
brothers and sisters, did they

push Phoenician prows, billowing those
huge wing-like sails, the same winds
bending our chrysanthemums, did they

blow past the first herd of blue whales
rounding arctic glaciers out to
    sea in
        search of krill, albatross wing-feathers
fluttered by their
    breezes, the

same ones rattling
   loose things in our
yard,

or do winds die, does air die, as all things
seem to, does space actually
die, the reverse of the way it is said it

came to birth in the Big Bang, not into an
   already existing space, but being

space itself actually expanding with all the
matter that would ever be stretching
   out in its flashing mesh, but does it then
die as well, do these
   winds, after turning some
intricate cyclonic circles around our

houses and selves, ruffling
hair and grass equally, do they

go off somewhere like lumbering
elephants to die, perhaps

far out at sea, alone, in the
   dark?

(Can we imagine a wind dying in daylight,
among people walking along the
coastline during their
lunch-break?)

But rather, rounding a huge hunch of
blackness, out past the

thrums of earth's immediate
atmosphere, the winds'

burial ground, flat and
silent, plain and vast, unutterably

quiet, the last

trickles of turbulence coming as if last
threads of wind snuggling under a rug of featureless space,
being space itself, rolling over

one last time and dying!

It all comes from the Book
and goes back into the
Book again.

"Everything perishes, except Allah's Face."

Wind too then, air, and us, and

space.

6/14 – 6/23

THE QUEST FOR BEAUTY

A green thought in a green shade
— Andrew Marvel

1

Humans love to walk slowly down the aisles of their
      local nurseries
looking at plants, smelling them, picking out
ones they want to take home to put in their
houses or plant in their gardens, to watch them
thrive, grow, fruit and
      flower, put out
shoots, surround with

garden perspectives, catch
sunlight, dwell in
      shade, inviting, in the slow

buzz of a summer afternoon.

We love to surround ourselves with earthly
greenery. Is it the

smell, the color,
    slim stems and
        new leaves? Is it a
memory of the
dark loaminess of the womb, a
loving leaf-mold premonition of the

grave? Our
arterial connection to
vines and nervous
    roots, reaching for
a handhold on the
nutritiously stabilizing earth, dream of
        material permanence, to

be flourishing through seasons,
unflinchingly witnessing
seasonal changes, pushing our

roots in deeper? Is it a

seedy green witness to our
sexual natures, extension of live
animal into silently twitching
vegetable, those

anonymous and
humble creatures bordering our
patios and lawns, swaying us to

more gradual wisdoms? Or is it a

flat-out memory of the pre-creational
Garden we've all ventured from in
this life, with its hints of
    sweet aromas of the supra-
intoxicating kind, where we went

drunkenly among greenery as in a tropical
dream, our own

touch aligning with delicate
shiverings of plant and tree,

lanes in public parks, secret
hills full of cactus and exotic herbage,
sudden pyrotechnics of the naturally unfolding
	spectrum,

jeweled miracles of orchids, the symbolically perfect
	passionflower
with its stamen cross and fringe-crown of thorns,
outrageously slug-like succulents, generous fruit-trees,
unstoppable tenacity of vines, whisperings above all

of all these growing things become like
loose harp-strings for breezes –

we walk with silent others in the aisles at the
local nursery plotting our personal
return to that first Garden via a few
well-placed pots of geraniums, hanging
cascades of scarlet fuchsias, splash of

water-spouts, spray of
	hose-nozzles,

"Annihilating all that's made
To a green thought in a green shade."

2

So that it's
out of a garden

radiance comes,
cutting out outlines of

forms and
flowers with

pencil-thin rays making spokes around them,
living representations of idea-like

manifestations of Allah's
Presence in Absence,

spaces in between stems and the
stems themselves,

we move among pots with dirt in our fingernails,
lining up our

centers with invisible
centrifugal uncoilings of

plants. So that
as we pat soil around the

base of a newly planted
plant, is it we who are

planting, or we who are getting
planted? Having joined up that

green mentality, soothing all our
actions smooth, to

gingerly lift up a new plant so
easily bruised, not wanting to

jeopardize its
blooms?

Shadows and light fall
upon us

equally. With a
trowel in hand, and

baggy shirt, slowing
down to the

rhythm of the
earth itself

breathing,
taking a new shoot into its soil,

as we will be
soon taken in, alone, to

grow.

We have to come to terms with
beauty before we die. We have to

look it in the face. At the last
perfect moment, the

bullet's nose
closing in, radiating

exquisite patterns of symmetry like magnetic lace
zeroing in on us. All the way out to

the stars. We are a
single seed falling

diagonally through
space. Going

home. Having

bloomed to its
extreme, influenced the

rest by our
scent or

shape, having
given off seed in our

going, now
encased in our genetic archetype once and for all

from field of action to
field of meaning

to see what secret
flower represents our

place.

Until Light ambles through the
Garden

dispensing Grace.

3

We plant great and terrible things in the garden of the earth
and they plant us.

We plant apartheid in South Africa, and it
in turn plants white supremacists in the
beginning rumble of the
avalanche of their downfall, so that
what began as a neat expediency soon becomes
a frantic death-dance on an oiled dance floor.

We plant splitting the atom as our source of energy,
radiant light of it surrounding our
power with an unearthly halo, and it
plants us deep in intoxicated soil, earth itself becomes
drunk on forbidden wine, nuclear

waste can't be
disposed of without disposing of
      us instead, reindeer
die from the lichen they've eaten for
      centuries, Laplanders
            have to
move from their embroidered yurts, the
ones that survived, to
cement-block houses facing
   a blank wall of a blank sky.

We plant tyrants in the earth to help us in
strategic places on the
earth, and they practice such
unpardonable atrocities on their people
            they have to be
forcibly removed, sometimes not
budging until the
      entire garden itself be
      ploughed up or
            left to go to seed,

we plant great and terrible things in the garden of the earth,
and they plant us,

we plant a shining road of spirituality
between dark mountains of hard matter

that has for its asphalt
songs of the heart, and this
      road

plants us, we rise
out of our
bed of packed earth to

breathe fresh air and unfold
flower and fruit of
divine accomplishment, we plant

our own selves deep in the
dark and
nurture them, and

wait for the correct balance of
water and earth
to wake us,

in the garden of the
earth we plant

and the planting
plants us, and the Light of

God trans-

plants us.

4

At the very moment of my writing this
the inventory of plants actually in my care

beyond the three human family members, two cats and one
    cockatiel who is
in my care more than anyone's, the plants from
the plant kingdom sharing their
        green destiny with
me are: One tomato plant still in its
strange net-covered earth-clump in a
plastic container, packet from
Wendy's Hamburgers given to
small children, usually ended up
        tended by adults, I

opened the thing that looked like what
jelly comes in at the
restaurant, added
    water until it
first bloated up, then pushed down the visible
seeds as instructed and soon it
started putting forth tender shoots, and now the
plant is five or six stems on the
    windowsill, and I put
    finger-dribbles of cold water from the
tap onto the
soil each day, and lately have said
        each day to our
daughter to remind her
mother (the better gardener) to take it
    into the back garden and
put it in the
ground, *"Or it's a goner"* —

one Venus flytrap, purchased this very weekend
at the Home Improvement Center, always
 wanted a Venus flytrap, it's got
five stems with
nearly translucent green cross-toothed pod-heads,
can't really call them
flowers, one
 greedily open, two
clamped shut with a
  dark bug or something already
   trapped inside them, we
bought it that way, presumably
 digesting their
  dinner and will fall open again
   perhaps with a
vegetal burp when
 finally finished, and on two
slender stems two miniscule
fledgling chompers deftly uncurling, not yet
 able to
  snap, I keep the
peat-moss stuff wet in its
plastic container, we take it
out onto the
patio table occasionally to keep the
 fly population down while we
  eat, but so far
not one fly is fool enough to
walk into its jaws, which, the
 salesgirl assured us, have a
particularly hard-to-resist gummy substance

inside them, thus far
   resisted;

and thirdly, a
hanging plant over the
bird-cage the cockatiel eats leaves from when he can
reach, in spite of
   my wife's protestations, she's the real

gardener in the family, has the
mystique about it down, ambling around in the
sun getting her
   fingers in the dirt, and is the one who suggested the
title *"Quest For Beauty"* for this
sequence as the
real motivation for love of
   plants, although conceded I might have,
in the first part, pinpointed what that
Quest is all about, memories either
      past or future of Paradise,
and it was
she also who felt it should be
   stressed how
working with
plants is so
purifying, centers you, empties you and

fills you again with clean

mindfulness.

5

Leaves the size of
pieces of sky like

transparent green
veils you think you

might see the Face of God through but you
only see sunlight,

gold sieved through these
leaves in

slanted rays,

that call us
to the Garden.

Stillness in shadow, not even
holding its

breath, but
bated, air being

circulated by
cells and sent

out as
oxygen, slim

turbines of a heavenly energy so
powerful it could

turn mountains into
small mounds of earth around the

base of the smallest plant,

that
calls us
to the Garden.

Shadows crisscrossed by vanilla light, webs of
light like slung

hammocks between
trees, jungle

crouchedness ready to
spring, quiet before

outburst, vegetable muteness before
riot, jabber one

moment exploding from the
vegetable core, so that

growing things actually
speak to us,

call us

to the Garden,

like dolphins diving nose-down into waves,
showing

only so much of their
being to our

prying eyes, the green
plant-world vouchsafing us

unshy glances at its
most delicate inner petals, most

intimate fleshy lusciousness,
but it's a

multicolored mask and diversion from their
secret harmony with air and earth,

water and fire, the
wood of their slow

thinking catching
fire and floating down the

waters of the
earth to the

oceans of a single consciousness,

that calls us
to the Garden.

Leaves inter-
weave and leave us

alive among
chlorophyll

crispness,
dots of golden light-spores are blazing suns as they

float into air
to take

root in
new

soil, flutter as
slow as tide-change, and as

sure, calling us both
forward and

back
to the Garden we

belong in,
Garden of our

true home,

breathing among

its softly
brandishing

blades.

6/25 – 6/30

THERE'S SOMETHING SO TOUCHING

There's something so touching in hearing
flutes and piccolos
imitating birds, they are

not birds, no bird would
probably be fooled, they are shrill human

approximations, then the
cellos and strings come up under them, waves,
wind-currents, programmatic

rollings of thunderous tones, to fold together watery

rushes of sound like the
waters coming back together again over the
armies of the Pharaoh.

Something so final, something born out of natural
wonder, a phenomenon of
   nature, cataract of
      ocean, or shaped
wood making a cello cat-gut is
pulled across and bowed to emit an
almost human sound, as if
     singing, but
   richer, and more
        sustained, put the

human voice above it, above a

solo cello, and what might happen could
extend the sound of

nature doubled and going into
infinitely multiplied resonance,

buzz of hornet in from the garden this afternoon,
following us around, attracted to our
colors or smells, then trying to
bat it out the sliding door-windows with a
broom, successfully, it flew right back

in again, visiting us on its
rounds, in nature's
   wrong rooms, then
out again, the
sound, of its wings? Of some
   clattering gills in its
     plates? Of the
plates themselves? Making such a

high-pitched warning, as of our
   brother the
mosquito whom I kill without
compunction, their
sins displayed in the
   blood-red
     liquid on the
wall for
all to see, but their

buzz, in the
night, waking us
up out of dead sleep, it's (in their

case at least) the
   needle-nose vibrating like a
      dentist's drill to
soften the victim's
skin for the
plunge, as Allah has taken care of

everything in
nature, and it is all so

inimitable, and our

imitation of it is primitive
ritual, linking us with

  forces and
     songs beyond our
God-given natures, but acknowledging

our meshed place in God's given
creation, sometimes

fishing freely in its
waves and

sometimes
caught.

7/4

I HAD A BRIEF INTIMATION TONIGHT

I had a brief intimation tonight of the
    place I write this
brain-flash heart stuff, not
obscured by water-faucets, dust, having to
    get up, get out, get back, take the
        garbage out, nor

these particular walls, sounds, darknesses, interruptions,

but a sunken room with no books in it, no
  shelves, no one
else's words strung together in
    any way, and either

high up overlooking the city at night far away
down below it with its
starry street-light twinkles, but so

far away as to be
    totally silent, there is a
      curving away at
          either side of my
peripheral vision of pale
    blue walls, going almost

infinitely out at
either side to where it
no longer matters, and there is the

great plate-glass window, also curved, and the room is
cut off from the
    rest of the
        house, perched on a
    hillside, or else

upside-down to the night somewhere near where
owls live and hunt, in a
    woods so deep you hear the
  great almost clumsy flap of their
wings as they
    swoop on prey, upside-

down to the night, a room that is
  so impenetrably
deep in the
    heart of nature it has become

super-nature, at an
    opposite pole, and the
arc-light of electricity jumping between them

is the room I write these
odes to the Unknown in, and the

splatter of lights cleaves our
    ego in two in one
        burst, we are left

naked and yawning as an arroyo in the
dark with its

dry mouth of shale turned up

as wide as it can

trying to drink stars!

7/6

SUMMER NIGHT

> *"Know that man in this world is dead-alive, and in the Next*
> *World he will be alive-dead. We said dead-alive in this world*
> *because in this world authority belongs to his death over his life.*
> *We said alive-dead in the Next World because in the Next World*
> *his life rules his death. In this world the dominant judgment is*
> *life. Man is dead alive, and will be alive dead."*
> — Shaykh Ali al-Jamal *(The Meaning of Man)*

Summer night,
   heat like a delirium,
hum of plastic electric fan on swivel
      so no corner goes uncooled,
thinking of all the *"Voyage"* or
"Invitation to the Voyage" poems written by
various Rimbauds, Baudelaires, Whitman with his
taking to the Open Road,

dark gray rafters like a wall across my sight
go up like hinged girders on a suspension bridge
and the desire for the thing, the actual

gas of desire to set off into an Unknown with
nothing but a kind of chromatic emptiness and
symphonic tone of impetus to undertake
what has begun with no particular
   lever or direction and has a
      soul's terrible desire to pass down

something like the Amazon with
examples from every *Kubla Khan*

pleasure dome
phantasmal rendezvous station, glass
       pavilions with dragons of
           scarlet ice hovering
               above them, railroad
stations in Siberia with blankets of
powder-blue fog filling space through which a
mournful whistle and
       escape of steam can be
hauntingly heard, the rounding of a

bend into totally visceral tropics, like creature-
nerves exuded from the
       vegetal natures of our
           very humanity, things that
glisten and curl, things that
hang and waver, dark brown lights with
       ochre centers, burnished
gold moths making slow arcs over
           dead black water,
snort and sniffle of deep-throated water creatures
       about to submerge out of
           sight, the

detailed abundance that would
     bite and scratch and finally
swallow us whole if we were
       actually there, then the

waterway opens and we're in geometrical
architectural smoothness of a Babylonia as

pictured by visionary archeologists, sand-yellow
walls going straight up, stairways on
    sheer cliff-like buttresses, terraces
leading to higher
    terraces, occasional
wingéd beast busts looming out of cantilevers,
pillars holding up canopy-like
    stucco roofs, processionals
        beneath them, un-
    noticing as we
            pass, having

stumbled backwards in
time on our
forward journey,

Siam now, the pillars slimmer and shining with
bright yellow gold-leaf, too
    bright, just
    applied, giant
beneficent faces everywhere at all the

corners of the
buildings, an almost

edible compassion to matter, matter as
spires of mental habitableness,

mental world wondrously created for the
peace beyond mentality to well
    up in, edges and

latticework topknots of
    towers almost
meshing in the
    sky like gears, and down slow-

currented canals our browless
barge goes forward, floating on its
own, forced by the

jags of my imaginings as I sit in
anticipation for more of the
unexpected to fill this
page, out of a
pen-point zigzagging almost on its
own, going nose-first into

Africa, dust, yellow dust rising, yellow dust settling,
scrubby dry trees on a wide flat horizon, and voices

blending consonants and vowels in a way never
    heard before, as if out of
        China, four-tonal African
lingo rapidly
enunciated in the
boiling heat, it seems it could

not be about bus-tickets or the price of
nails, but has to be a language picked up from
the observations for centuries of
    animal migrations,
        flash of tropical

                    birds in
flight, shadows on
        calabash,
    scent of
    hibiscus as the
            first sign of
                Spring, the
earth shaking,
    lightning's eloquence,
    the words cracks of lightning
            actually say,

out of the pure hearts of men and women, words of that
purity, vocal hieroglyphics in motion
on the black expanses from this millisecond

back to the beginning and
forward to the
end, with the

first concerns in our hearts given the
deft-footed vocabulary of immediacy
and praise, like

fish-hooks of the
    Creator let
down into the
waters of the
world via our

poles to catch

meanings before they
swim back to the
unifying sea.

2

One step, two.
Chalk wind blows past,
    pencil lines
scribbled in it. Tearing at my
    hair. Jetting the
        tail of my
coat out at an acute
angle. Has

anyone ever gone anywhere?

We step out. One step. Two. As
teenagers with pimples or without we
want desperately to
get out of what has been a
nuclear cocoon and
take to the open road as a matter of life or death,

we travel with black tassels on our patent leather shoes on board
1920's ocean liners, being millionaires, and if we
don't go down with the Titanic we live to have
giggled late at night on the
boozy expatriate boulevards of Paris and then

sit in fuzzy nobility years later reminiscing to
awed grandchildren, or methodically
write our memoirs, but have we

actually gone anywhere at all with all our
efforts? Have the

crumbling dusts of Dead Sea Scrolls deposited their
powders on our fingertips or brows? Did we

even so much as open the giant
    volcanic eye in our
heads to catch a
        glimpse of the
wonder? To come back
complete strangers? Passing like

ghosts among the
self-satisfied dead?

Did we actually strap on the merest of baggage
with a squint-eyed guide between dark
houses at night, or fall into a

love so mighty it tore the
curtains from our natal house, tore even the walls and
windows off in its

silken tornado that leaves a
smoking black
hole in the

ground that
was ourselves. Crazed

love-notes hang on the points of the thorn bush,
and a scandalous fame
    outlasts us, echoing
        our
passion. Cryptic remarks

delivered in deadpan were the only
indications of a

road already rutted with ditches so
    deeply etched by the
wooden wheels of the
cart of Inevitability in our
    hearts that we could

barely speak. Pure white

letter-paper with a word or two
sprinkled on it and sent to its

intended seen only by
night-breezes going into
The Beloved's window

was actually
bleached skin

flayed from us

in ancient
Aztec ritual style
and flattened by
flat-irons of moonlight before being

kissed and put in an
envelope and dropped into any old
mailbox on any
street corner along with the
        gas bill.

Has anyone actually taken one
step forward

and not found that at the end of the
giant circle and seven continents and thirty foreign countries
later that the

self is a crocodile's shadow set up
    alongside our
        actions and
snapping its
    jaws at us when
least expected, and though we

would like to move on past its
swampy influence, our
feet are
        hopelessly
            entangled in the
Florida lianas that would

ensnarl us and
pull us in.

One step, and then a
second.

Mankind has taken many journeys from its
    center on this
        globe over the
millennia, Phoenicians out in their
catamarans, Napoleon into
Egypt, Alexander into
Afghanistan, Queen Victoria into
India and Africa, the white
    European onto the land of the Indian Tribes,
the white European onto the
        land of the Zulus,

until the criteria of justice and right are
the prerogative of English-speaking white men alone
and the dark races have to fight their
hearts out to get even a
square of their own
    land to
        themselves.

Voyage to the tap of an iron drumbeat, boot-heels hitting
and cutting through the earth's crust,

but has
anyone ever actually

taken the journey and come

back from
 behind the clouds that veil
the peak of the hill?

It's all been in the blink of an eye.

The outgoing and the
incoming. One

breath held for less than a
 minute
contains the
 topography, the
map, the
actual railroad lines, and the

goal. But unless we
started out, we can't be
 said to
arrive, and

unless we take the
journey we

won' t have
traveled.

One step, then
two. To find ourselves

purified
where we
began.

As if standing still in the instant that is our lives, the
journeys, the comings and
goings, formed one symmetrical

wheel with unfolding petals spinning
out from the
    center of our
        stationary
stance,

and every bend or shrug or
smile of joy
were the messages
those petals contained

and the dazzling growth in seven-dimensional
space beyond our
own personal deaths were the

actual invisible movement of our
limbs in the
one voyage taken beyond our
control, that

leads us and
beckons us

on.

3

In waking we can choose to go
deep undersea to pearls or in the
    sky to take pictures of the
        whole earth at a
glance, or voyage to
    Mars to live in
        infrared light eating
rust-bitter lichens rubbed from iron-red rock,

but in dream we have no choice, we have to
    stand in the crowded restaurant where our
mother and father calmly walk in naked and
    order pastrami sandwiches much to our
helpless embarrassment until we go out the
        pyramid's door onto a
            flat desert with
                blue palm trees, the camels all
passing at the
bottom of a silver lake, their
humps reflected in
purple clouds hovering overhead,

we answer to our
name bubbling through the air,

waking we can choose to

dream our voyage, tied to the
mast past the
        bewildering sirens, or we can
choose to subject these one-time bodies to
    incredible hardships, trudging with
        blue toes to the top of the North Pole or
the sheer needle-narrow peak of
            Anapurna, we can

choose to drop out of an airplane
    with or without a
parachute

(and just tonight I saw on
television a *"That's Incredible"* episode of a
soldier in training doing a parachute jump but his
main parachute flew off him, his second one
went up twisted and didn't open, his last-
ditch third emergency parachute
            tangled up in the
                    second, he was
hurtling earthward, saw
            houses, TV aerials, back gardens, all
        rushing up to meet him, then
everything slowed down to
unfathomable slow-motion, just as it
did for me in Colima, Mexico, in 1966 as I
flew out the back rumble-seat of a
        Thunderbird as it
            rolled off the shoulder and went
sailing up in the air then

straight along toward a dazzling sheet of light
if I went through I knew I'd die, but
    pressed against it then
      fell back to earth, in
incredible slow-motion until
   black-out at impact, immediately
conscious again with broken
   pelvis and right elbow, adrenalin pumping, calling out
to the one safe and sound friend, a track-star
who landed running on his feet, to
please get me my glasses and black fountain-pen,

so this guy comes straight down thinking, he said, of the
times he wondered what other
guys he'd seen die like this had thought as
last thoughts, then he
landed full force on a front lawn in
   suburbia, numb and
     immediately amazed to be
        still alive, euphoric but immobile, probably
80% of the
bones in his
     body broken in
   hundreds of places, he survived and went on to
       dive again,

waking and dream both, choice and
       no-choice, the
   clock of destiny catching him in its
      tick and
     letting him go)

but we set out with an intention and are
deflected in the tropics eating
bananas in hammocks or

handed a bag of hot diamonds as we
stand on a street corner in Rome and then get sent to
jail for jewel theft.

Dreaming or awake, we live in the
houses of our bodies inhabiting the
attic or the cellar, or all the
        rooms at once, it

gets up in its shape, walks out a door into
bronze sunlight, looks through
        intelligent eyes into
other intelligent eyes, with

larynx and tongue and innumerable
teeth says what the
        spirit in its
            state dictates, we

walk toward a ramp, or through a
door or to a
chair, or lie down on a

bed, in a room, in
silence, in the
dark, to
dream

the solid awakening into Allah's
manipulations that we need only
see in motion to see the

intentions He has for us,

circling back again to the song of the Voyage,
taking to the
    Open Road of the
        Closed System,

singing the *Song of Return*

as we

set out.

4

Because the journey that we take is
    really beyond death
in which we don't wake up in
    this world
        but the
            Next.

It starts out at our boot-heels all right, it
begins at the cut-out shape we make
    where we are right
        now, standing or

        sitting or
lying on our sides, quiescent or in
     action, compassionate or
        frantic, it starts at the
glance we take above our
      own noses, seeing the
shadow-flesh-image of our
noses just slightly, ghostly, in our
          gaze,

it begins with this thought, and
that one, and shoots in a
clear light path directly to our
place after death, the
exact location! Grave was just

clothes, a strict
  formal suit of
winding-sheet and
  earth to let us
while away our
   time in
bliss of green contemplation of The Garden or
hair-raising terror of The Fire with our
ribs crushed together, but only a

formal suit of clothes, with serious-minded
worms in the pockets, but it
didn't concern us, because the

true voyage catapults us past it, into the

spotlit clarity of extra-worldly delights, where
the passport is God's Mercy and the
dignity of our case, to go down

flowery hillsides among the
fountains of eternal delirium,

or boiled like a fish with its
cracked lips making an
   "O" forever, and
wide blank eyes.

No suit of clothes
needs us there. The

voyage has come
full round.

The flag bursts into
flame and is a

rose.

The rose

is the calling of our name.

7/7 – 7/11

THE DARKNESS IS A TENT OF MERCY

The darkness is a
    tent of mercy
  dropped down
        over our day.

In which to move
    furniture, as I have
        just done, shouldering
heavy bookcases full of books, by which I mean
shoving them ever so
    slowly into place with my
        shoulder, pivoting
the tall thin one around on its
    axis, consciously
going down into my
        body and
relaxing so as not to exert any unnecessary
  energy while all the
        rest of the house
sleeps, it being

past midnight,
coaxing the repainted now Chinese-like ox-blood
  cabinet with the pagoda-on-a-cliff figured
        enamel door-handles into
place under the
photograph of the Moroccan Shaykh looking straight
    out at you so that later I notice

everything in that corner shifted around and
moved to a new location but him, he stayed where he
was before, *unwobbling*
        pivot, and I

remembered, in shoving tall
bookcase with more than a
        hundred books still
                in it, the

Taoist story of the butcher of whom the
        Emperor asked the
secret of the
        grace & speed of his
                ability and he
poured out a clear and
joyful explanation of having the same unsharpened
blade for twenty years straight, he just makes sure
        when it
                cuts it meets
no resistance, it cuts
between not *into*,
        so that when he's

done he looks about with happy
accomplishment, having simply

moved with the energy of the
moment inside the
        already grooved grain of the
                beast he was

carving up,

and now
everything is in place. Night is for
    this. Then it is for the

phantom reversal of all this, mystical
night-stairs ascending
while the
    rest of the
        house
           sleeps,

all of day's too-bright hard-edged pictures
with their
    individuated leaves on
        Latin-named trees, or
the trillion errands flesh is heir to during
daylight hours, night throws its

mantle of mercy lightly over the skeletal
struts and flexions of our
    beings enough that
in a unified general pitch black sea
ever so invisibly we might
    step out of ourselves into
        another sunlight,

another reflection
    of rose-bushes and
passing clouds, in which

transformation takes place in the
    instant of a
        drop of water on
            silver, and the
glare is
overpowering, forcing us to

retreat back into the night

fallen around us with its
one cloth

enfolded in

impenetrable light.

7/16

THROUGH THE LATTICEWORK

Through the latticework
of a T'ang Dynasty balcony

shadows of horses fall blue
against glaring white snow.

Stutter of shadows as the whole cavalry passes.
Two tiny children's faces

flat against intricate carving look
through wide ornate openings.

Red cheeks. A whole dynasty
passes in the

flutter of blue shadows, snow then
a green hillside, brown grass, then

snow again.

The faces have become an old man and an old woman
who never married, may have been

brother and sister, sitting
at tea

on a teakwood balcony.
He of ancient lineage, neck stiff in

worked brocade. She,
younger but wrinkled,

swathed in
raw silk.

Two white rice-biscuits
in a white porcelain bowl.

They get very old and one day, a few hours apart,
die. Moths

fly out across the
moonlit hill,

tiny fluttering shadows on a
blue hillside.

7/20

SILENCE

1

I don't think anyone has ever
really experienced silence

but the one in whom the whole
universe disappears in a
   dot of light and then
also disappears and then the
     dot of light
       disappears!

But the rest of us, all the
rest of us, even the ones with the

lights out late at night in a
space shuttle, weightless, drifting,
   dark, the few
instrument-panel lights
soundlessly blinking just to show it's all
    keeping going,

even they haven't really experienced pure
silence. Asleep, the
palladiums of our atoms uncase their
   crystal diamond domes to a
careless, symmetrical
     hum, as even the

thin stems of flowers at night in the
  woods around
  redwood trees do, they also

hum the same tone, their atoms also lift their
    lids or
split spectrally down the
  middle like lunar
      oranges, and in a

shaft of light as
pure as if it
  came
straight from the
    moon,

the naked wedges also
  hum, and their
hum is in
    harmony with the
hub, and the

axle of all things turns from that
  hub through every
hubbub of manifestation to

point to a silence conceivable but

never perfectly achieved.

The sound of her breathing

next to me in the
    bed,

a distant
dog-bark.

2

Perhaps the silence of the eyelids closing for the
    last time, or the actual
silence of the
     spirit as it leaves the
body's captivity, or the

silence of the last flake of snow on a
    snowdrift as the
storm abates, just before the
bright quiet takes over, or the

silence of fingerprints being transferred from
killer to evidence just before
abandoning the scene, the silence of

frightened parachuters just before their
jump, deep sea divers just before

submerging to hunt for
treasure on the
wreck, the silence of

wood-ticks in twenty years' hibernation until animal
heat passes near them, the silence of

alpine flowers just after
   bursting into
bloom in
     pale sunlight, the

silence of a father who has gone past
grief for the
    first time after
      news of his
oldest son's death. The silence at the

bottom of the sea which is
actually interiorized sound, like
    depths in
contemplation, the

silence just after birth when you sink into
the localized blessing of
angelic activity for your

first nap outside the
    womb,

a silence that is not silent but like a
    preamble, the
taste of a
total unreachable

silence
to come.

3

Silent as an old tooth in a
bottle on a

museum shelf,
silent as drawers of skulls of actual people who once

walked around and
cracked nuts with their teeth, got

erections or rubbed their breasts, thought
nostalgically of their

childhoods, silent as

skeletons still in the ground, silent as all the
valuable antique

treasures and scrolls
still buried in the ground, everything

just underground, waiting to be discovered and unearthed, as
Troy was before Schliemann had his

methodical visions,

silent as animals in the
tundra in the

dead of winter,
silent as the

spider must be for hours on end
in the center of his

web —

I started by saying nothing is silent but what takes place
outside the

laws of this world, everything
whirrs or

clicks or
makes tiny bell-like tones just by

occupying space, then
out came an onslaught of things that seem

silent in their
way, sitting

facing us like the
faces of clocks, in

intermediary
worlds, or the silent space of a

pause between
thoughts which could be

a world in all its
populated entirety, ocean-rolls and

cloud pastures, spreading out
to infinity, a whisper emerging from

silence, last
words of a

Zen Master sitting in the
posture of death,

but these silences are just downbeats to the following
upsurge of sizzling

orchestral effects of
angelic creation making

bells of resonance
flow from the

breaths of the brave, the halt
in self-doubt, the arrogant Atheist, the

stunned criminal, the starving
Ethiopian farmer only

a few months away from

former subsistence, the

intricate network of
our human panoply, each one of us

a crossroads of silence and
sound, each one of us carrying within us

the scream of
defiance or

grief, reaching
back in time to

more difficult
origins, or the

single-voiced choir of
jubilations coming out of

seemingly nowhere to grant us our
human space, Voice

lifted on
silver pulleys up out of our

own limitations to
connect with

comet-trails and
paths of

invisible stars, as well as
carriers of a silence so vast and

absolute entire
prehistoric dynasties are

buried just beneath its
surface, history with all its

grimaces and
brocades is just a

reflection in
passing on the

mirror-shine of its
glass, a silence that

gives birth to an awe before the Creator in which that
Silent Voice may be heard that gets all things

into motion and sets all things
in their

final places
at last.

7/23

AFTER READING THIS LAST POEM

After reading this
   last poem to a
poet friend today out in the
     back garden
surrounded by listening
potted plants on brick walls, he said he had

just that morning written a line he
liked that went something like,
"The irreducible frequency by which
   everything as we
know it takes
   shape," and I told him it

summed up the whole
book I have been writing in
one line, and then the

subject came up about how in most major
cosmologies initial creative
   sound is
primary, in Arabic it's
"kún fa yakun:
Be! And it is," creative

words uttered by
Allah, enough to create
me with my 48 years, moustache and beard, you with your
   hopes and

fears, or

FIAT of the
    Christians,
       OM of the
Hindus & Buddhists —

the whole

boat of

creation

rides on its

ineluctable

waves.

7/25

ABOUT THE AUTHOR

Born in 1940 in Oakland, California, Daniel Abdal-Hayy Moore's first book of poems, *Dawn Visions*, was published by Lawrence Ferlinghetti of City Lights Books, San Francisco, in 1964, and the second in 1972, *Burnt Heart/Ode to the War Dead*. He created and directed *The Floating Lotus Magic Opera Company* in Berkeley, California in the late 60s, and presented two major productions, *The Walls Are Running Blood,* and *Bliss Apocalypse*. He became a Sufi Muslim in 1970, performed the Hajj in 1972, and lived and traveled throughout Morocco, Spain, Algeria and Nigeria, landing in California and publishing *The Desert is the Only Way Out,* and *Chronicles of Akhira* in the early 80s (Zilzal Press). Residing in Philadelphia since 1990, in 1996 he published *The Ramadan Sonnets* (Jusoor/City Lights), and in 2002, *The Blind Beekeeper* (Jusoor/Syracuse University Press). He has been the major editor for a number of works, including *The Burdah* of Shaykh Busiri, translated by Shaykh Hamza Yusuf, and the poetry of Palestinian poet, Mahmoud Darwish, translated by Munir Akash. He is also widely published on the worldwide web: *The American Muslim, DeenPort*, and his own website: www.danielmoorepoetry.com; and poetry blog: www. ecstaticxchange.wordpress.com, among others. He is also currently literary editor for *Seasons Journal* and *Islamica Magazine*. The Ecstatic Exchange Series is bringing out the extensive body of his works of poetry (a complete list of published works on page 2).

POETIC WORKS by Daniel Abdal-Hayy Moore
Published and Unpublished
(many to appear in *The Ecstatic Exchange* Series)

Dawn Visions (published by City Lights, 1964)
Burnt Heart/Ode to the War Dead (published by City Lights, 1972)
This Body of Black Light Gone Through the Diamond (printed by Fred Stone, Cambridge, Mass, 1965)
On The Streets at Night Alone (1965?)
All Hail the Surgical Lamp (1967)
States of Amazement (1970)

Abdallah Jones and the Disappearing-Dust Caper (published by The Ecstatic Exchange/Crescent Series, 2006)
'Ala ud-Deen and the Magic Lamp
The Chronicles of Akhira (1981) (published by Zilzal Press with Typoglyphs by Karl Kempton, 1986)
Mouloud (1984) (A Zilzal Press chapbook, 1995)
Man is the Crown of Creation (1984)
The Look of the Lion (The Parabolas of Sight) (1984)
The Desert is the Only Way Out (completed 4/21/84) (Zilzal Press chapbook, 1985)
Atomic Dance (1984) (am here books, 1988)
Outlandish Tales (1984)
Awake as Never Before (12/26/84) (Zilzal Press chapbook, 1993)
Glorious Intervals (1/1/85) (Zilzal Press chapbook, ?)
Long Days on Earth/Book I (1/28 – 8/30/85)
Long Days on Earth/Book II (Hayy Ibn Yaqzan)
Long Days on Earth/Book III (1/22/86)
Long Days on Earth/Book IV (1986)
The Ramadan Sonnets (Long Days on Earth/Book V) (5/9 – 6/11/86) (Published by Jusoor/City Lights Books, 1996) (Republished as Ramadan Sonnets by The Ecstatic Exchange, 2005)
Long Days on Earth/Book VI (6-8/30/86)
Holograms (9/4/86 – 3/26/87)
History of the World (The Epic of Man's Survival) (4/7 – 6/18/87)
Exploratory Odes (6/25 – 10/18/87)

The Man at the End of the World (11/11 – 12/10/87)

The Perfect Orchestra (3/30 – 7/25/88) (Published by The Ecstatic Exchange, 2009)

Fed from Underground Springs (7/30 – 11/23/88)

Ideas of the Heart (11/27/88 – 5/5/89)

New Poems (scattered poems, out of series, from 3/24 – 8/9/89)

Facing Mecca (5/16 – 11/11/89)

A Maddening Disregard for the Passage of Time (11/17/89 – 5/20/90)

The Heart Falls in Love with Visions of Perfection (6/15/90 – 6/2/91)

Like When You Wave at a Train and the Train Hoots Back at You (Farid's Book) (6/11 – 7/26/91) (Published by The Ecstatic Exchange, 2008)

Orpheus Meets Morpheus (8/1/91– 3/14/92)

The Puzzle (3/21/92 – 8/17/93)

The Greater Vehicle (10/17/93 – 4/30/94)

A Hundred Little 3-D Pictures (5/14/94 – 9/11/95)

The Angel Broadcast (9/29 – 12/17/95)

Mecca/Medina Time-Warp (12/19/95 – 1/6/96) (Published as a Zilzal Press chapbook, 1996)

Miracle Songs for the Millennium (1/20 – 10/16/96)

The Blind Beekeeper (11/15/96 – 5/30/97) (Published 2002 by Jusoor/ Syracuse University Press)

Chants for the Beauty Feast (6/3 – 10/28/97)

You Open a Door and it's a Starry Night (10/29/97 – 5/23/98) (Published by The Ecstatic Exchange, 2009)

Salt Prayers (5/29 – 10/24/98) (Published by The Ecstatic Exchange,2005)

Some (10/25/98 – 4/25/99)

Flight to Egypt (5/1 – 5/16/99)

I Imagine a Lion (5/21 – 11/15/99) (Published by The Ecstatic Exchange, 2006)

Millennial Prognostications (11/25/99 – 2/2/2000) (Published by the Ecstatic Exchange, 2009)

Shaking the Quicksilver Pool (2/4 – 10/8/2000) (Published by The Ecstatic Exchange, 2009)

Blood Songs (10/9/2000 – 4/3/2001)

The Music Space (4/10 – 9/16/2001) (Published by The Ecstatic Exchange, 2007)

Where Death Goes (9/20/2001 – 5/1/2002) (Published by The Ecstatic Exchange, 2009)

The Flame of Transformation Turns to Light (99 Ghazals Written in English) (5/14 – 8/21/2002) (Published by The Ecstatic Exchange, 2007)

Through Rose-Colored Glasses (7/22/2002 – 1/15/2003) (Published by The Ecstatic Exchange, 2007)

Psalms for the Broken-Hearted (1/22 – 5/25/2003) (Published by The Ecstatic Exchange, 2006)

Hoopoe's Argument (5/27 – 9/18/03)

Love is a Letter Burning in a High Wind (9/21 – 11/6/2003) (Published by The Ecstatic Exchange, 2006)

Laughing Buddha/Weeping Sufi (11/7/2003 – 1/10/2004) (Published by The Ecstatic Exchange, 2005)

Mars and Beyond (1/20 – 3/29/2004) (Published by The Ecstatic Exchange, 2005)

Underwater Galaxies (4/5 – 7/21/2004) (Published by The Ecstatic Exchange, 2007)

Cooked Oranges (7/23/2004 – 1/24/2005 (Published by The Ecstatic Exchange, 2007)

Holiday from the Perfect Crime (1/25 – 6/11/2005)

Stories Too Fiery to Sing Too Watery to Whisper (6/13 – 10/24/2005)

Coattails of the Saint (10/26/2005 – 5/10/2006) (Published by The Ecstatic Exchange, 2006)

In the Realm of Neither (5/14/2006 – 11/12/06) (Published by The Ecstatic Exchange, 2008)

Invention of the Wheel (11/13/06 – 6/10/07)

The Sound of Geese Over the House (6/15 – 11/4/07)

The Fire Eater's Lunchbreak (11/11/07 – 5/19/2008) (Published by The Ecstatic Exchange, 2008)

Sparks Off the Main Strike (5/24/2008 – 1/10/2009)

Stretched Out on Amethysts (1/13/2009 –)

www.ingramcontent.com/pod-product-compliance
Lightning Source LLC
Chambersburg PA
CBHW020901090426
42736CB00008B/454